P9-CMK-655

GRAPHIC LIBRARY™

GRAPHIC SCIENCE

INVESTIGATING THE
SCIENTIFIC METHOD

WITH

MAX AXIOM™
SUPER SCIENTIST

4D An Augmented Reading Science Experience

by Donald B. Lemke | illustrated by Tod G. Smith and Al Milgrom

Consultant:
Leslie Flynn, PhD
Science Education, Chemistry
University of Minnesota
Twin Cities Campus

CAPSTONE PRESS
a capstone imprint

Graphic Library is published by Capstone Press,
1710 Roe Crest Drive, North Mankato, Minnesota 56003.
www.mycapstone.com

Library of Congress Cataloging-in-Publication Data is available on the Library of Congress website.

ISBN: 978-1-5435-5870-8 (library binding)
ISBN: 978-1-5435-6003-9 (paperback)
ISBN: 978-1-5435-5880-7 (eBook PDF)

Summary: In graphic novel format, follows the adventures of
Max Axiom as he explains the scientific method.

Art Director and
Designer
Bob Lentz

Cover Artist
Tod Smith

Colorist
Krista Ward

Editor
Christopher Harbo

Photo Credits
Capstone Studio: Karon Dubke, 29, back cover

1 Ask an adult to
download the app.

Capstone 4D
Education

2 Scan any page with the star.

3 Enjoy your cool stuff!

—— OR ——

Use this password at capstone4D.com

method.58708

Printed in the United States of America.
PA48

TABLE OF CONTENTS

SECTION 1 A WORLD OF QUESTIONS

Inside his high-tech laboratory, Super Scientist Max Axiom receives an important video message.

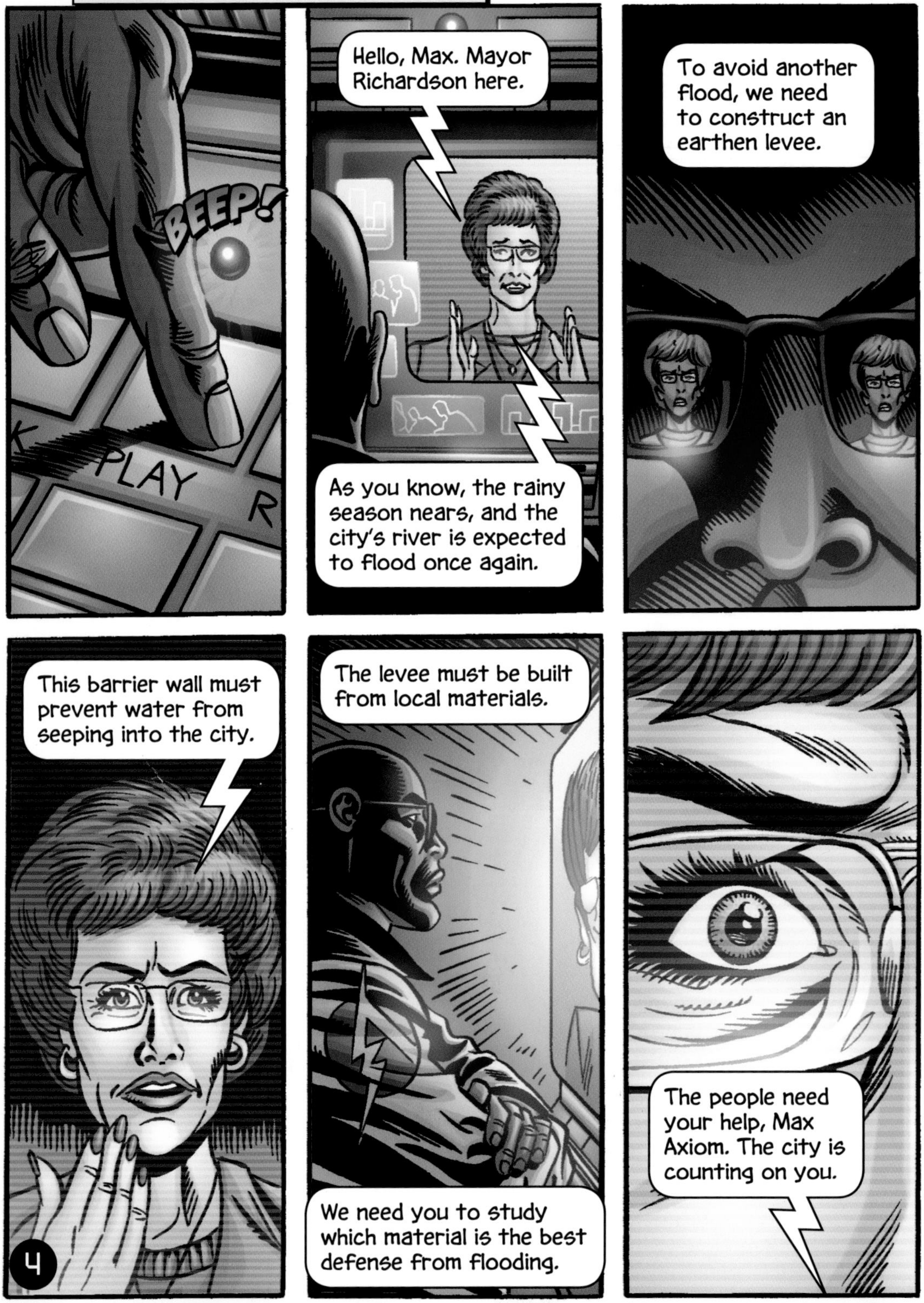
BEEP!
PLAY
Hello, Max. Mayor Richardson here.
As you know, the rainy season nears, and the city's river is expected to flood once again.
To avoid another flood, we need to construct an earthen levee.
This barrier wall must prevent water from seeping into the city.
The levee must be built from local materials.
We need you to study which material is the best defense from flooding.
The people need your help, Max Axiom. The city is counting on you.

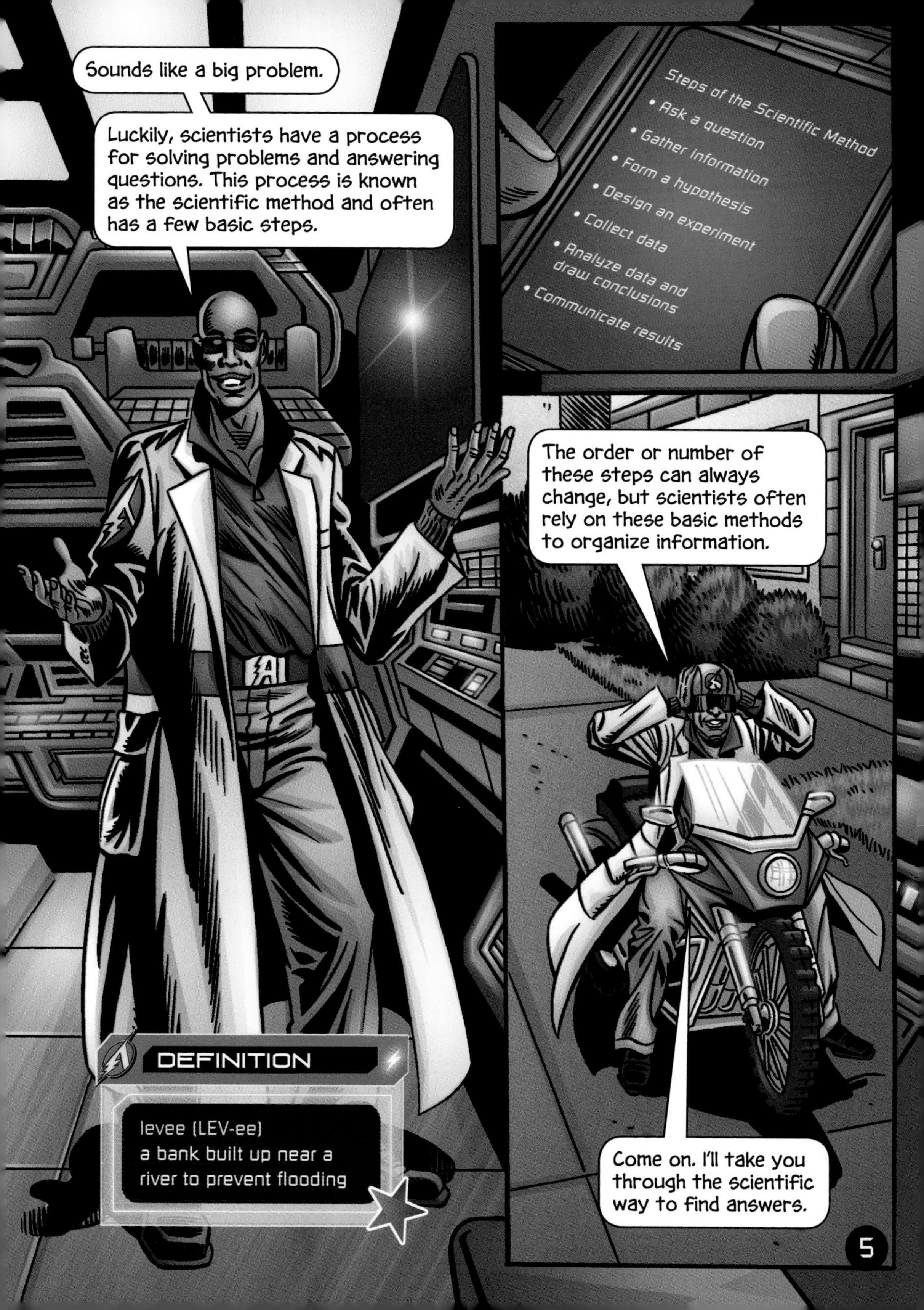
Sounds like a big problem.
Luckily, scientists have a process for solving problems and answering questions. This process is known as the scientific method and often has a few basic steps.
Steps of the Scientific Method
• Ask a question
• Gather information
• Form a hypothesis
• Design an experiment
• Collect data
• Analyze data and draw conclusions
• Communicate results
The order or number of these steps can always change, but scientists often rely on these basic methods to organize information.
DEFINITION
levee (LEV-ee)
a bank built up near a river to prevent flooding
Come on. I'll take you through the scientific way to find answers.

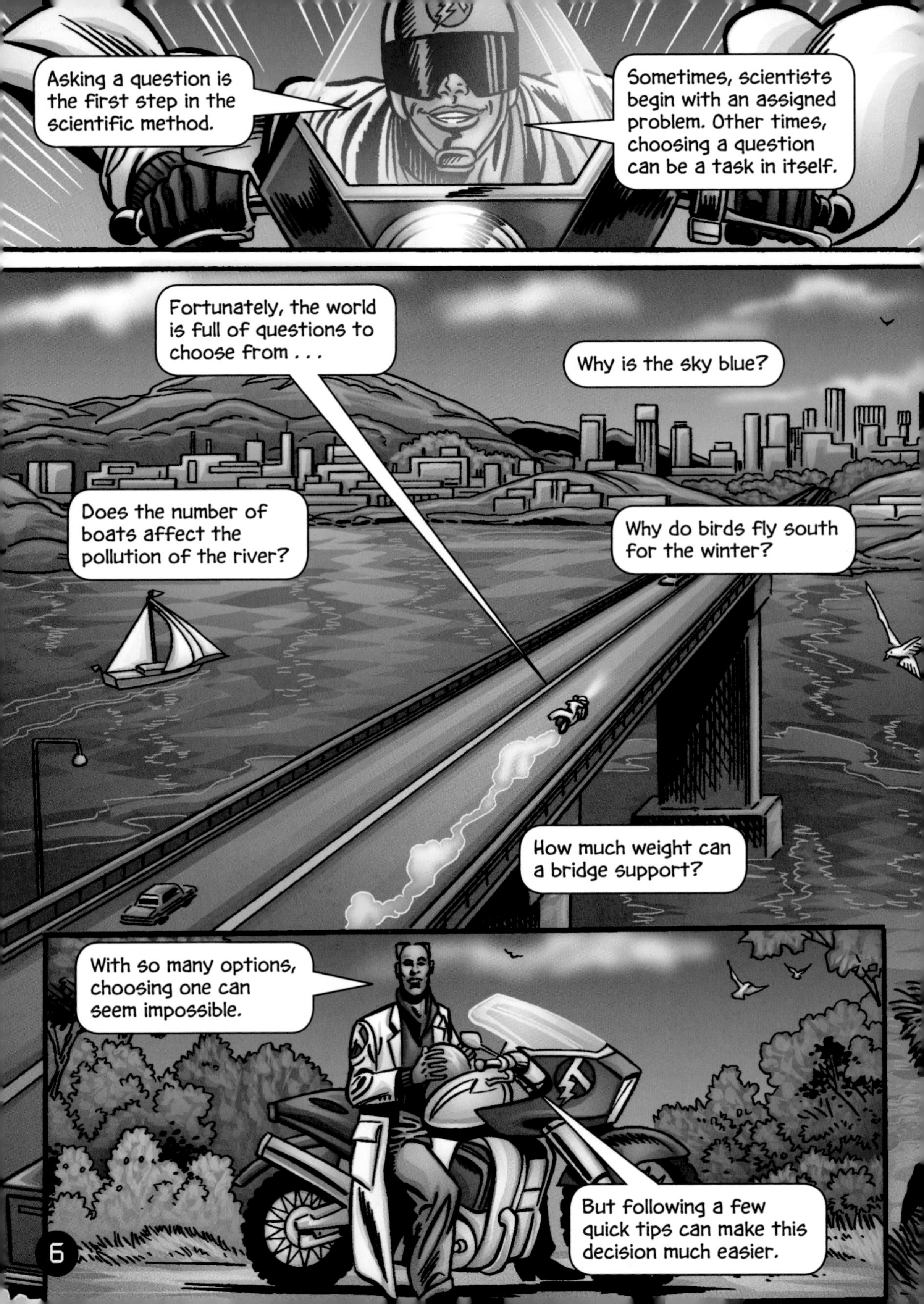

Asking a question is the first step in the scientific method.
Sometimes, scientists begin with an assigned problem. Other times, choosing a question can be a task in itself.
Fortunately, the world is full of questions to choose from . . .
Why is the sky blue?
Does the number of boats affect the pollution of the river?
Why do birds fly south for the winter?
How much weight can a bridge support?
With so many options, choosing one can seem impossible.
But following a few quick tips can make this decision much easier.

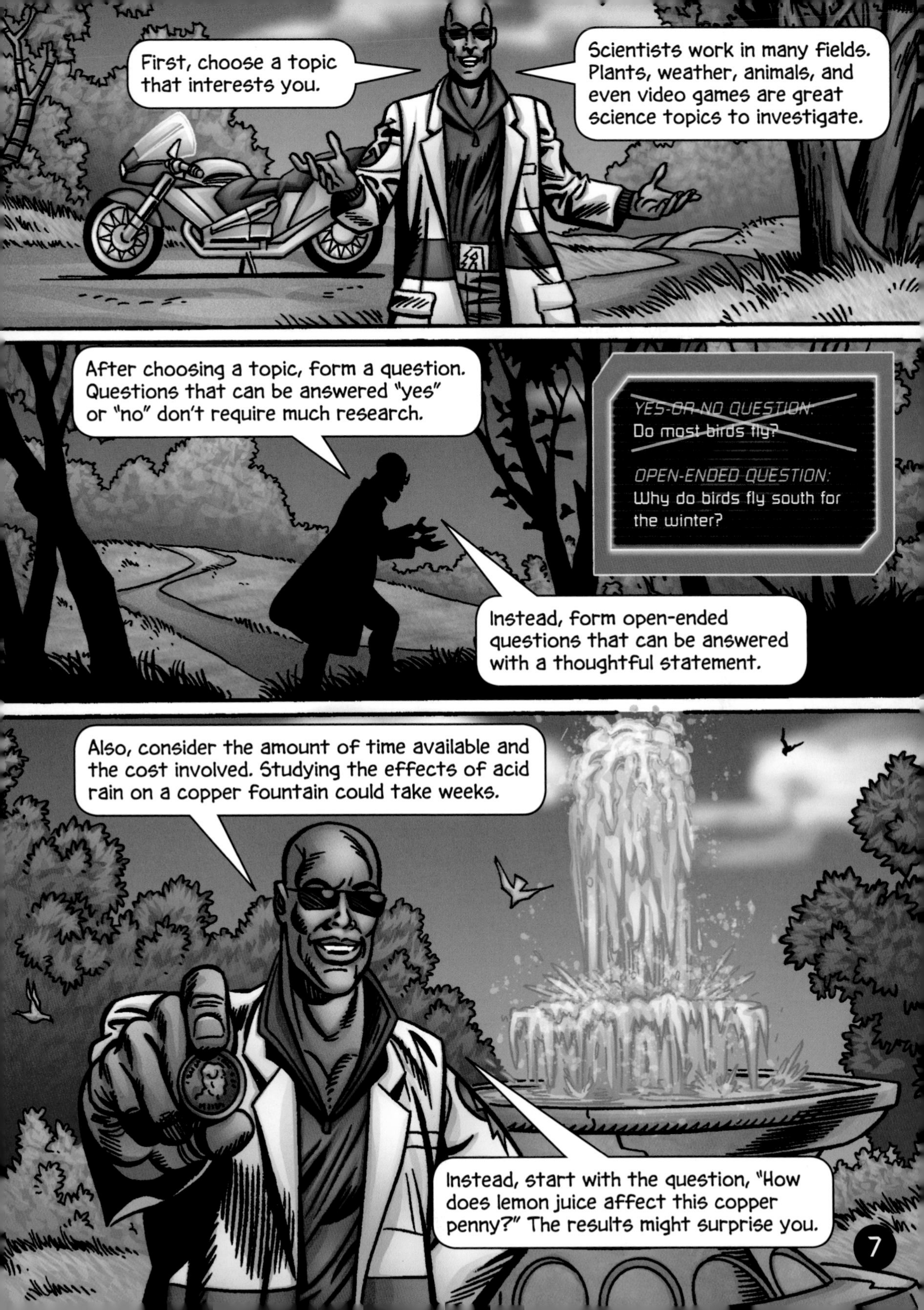
First, choose a topic that interests you.
Scientists work in many fields. Plants, weather, animals, and even video games are great science topics to investigate.
After choosing a topic, form a question. Questions that can be answered "yes" or "no" don't require much research.
YES-OR-NO QUESTION:
Do most birds fly?
OPEN-ENDED QUESTION:
Why do birds fly south for the winter?
Instead, form open-ended questions that can be answered with a thoughtful statement.
Also, consider the amount of time available and the cost involved. Studying the effects of acid rain on a copper fountain could take weeks.
Instead, start with the question, "How does lemon juice affect this copper penny?" The results might surprise you.

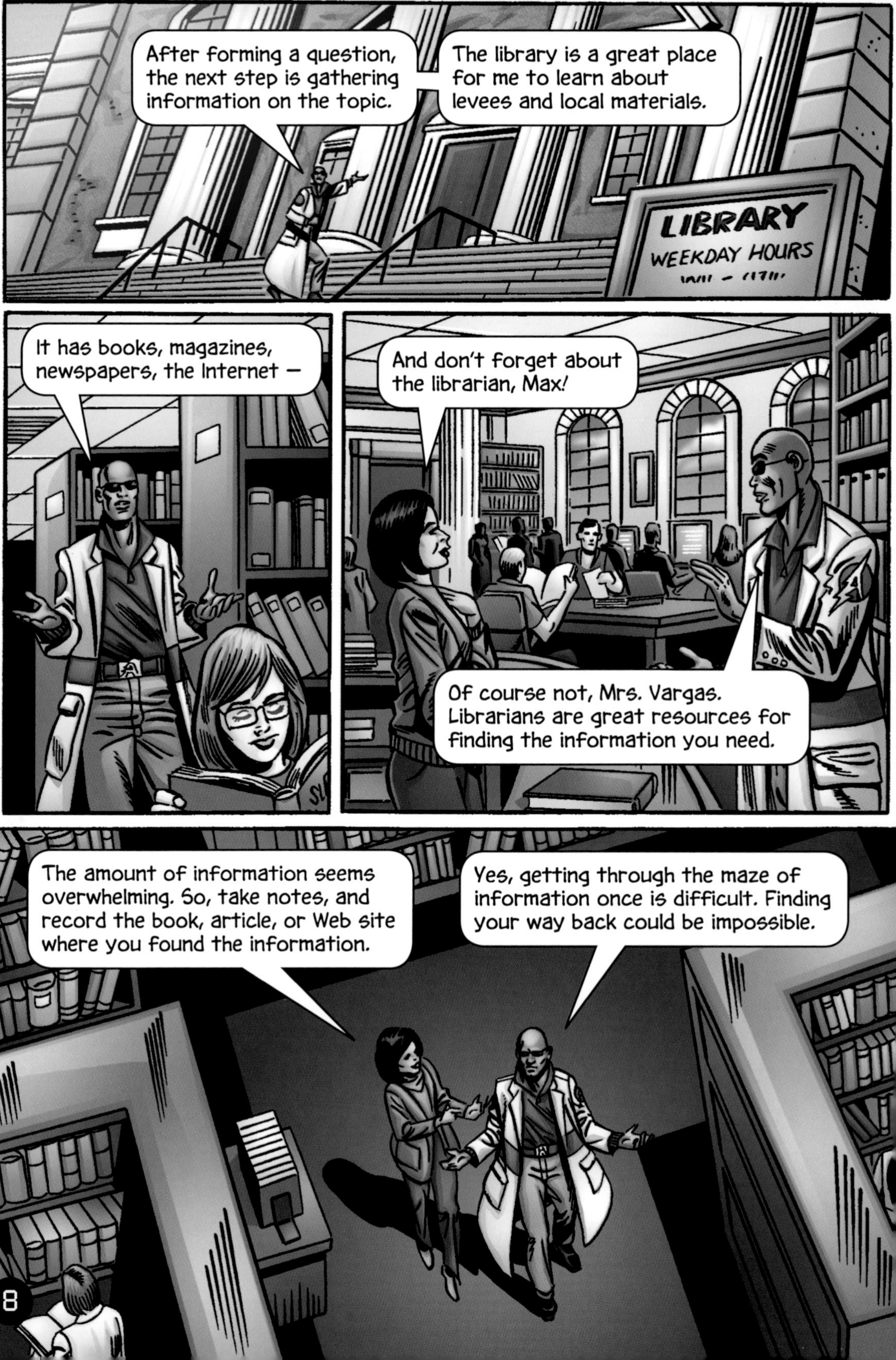
After forming a question, the next step is gathering information on the topic.
The library is a great place for me to learn about levees and local materials.
LIBRARY
WEEKDAY HOURS
It has books, magazines, newspapers, the Internet —
And don't forget about the librarian, Max!
Of course not, Mrs. Vargas. Librarians are great resources for finding the information you need.
The amount of information seems overwhelming. So, take notes, and record the book, article, or Web site where you found the information.
Yes, getting through the maze of information once is difficult. Finding your way back could be impossible.

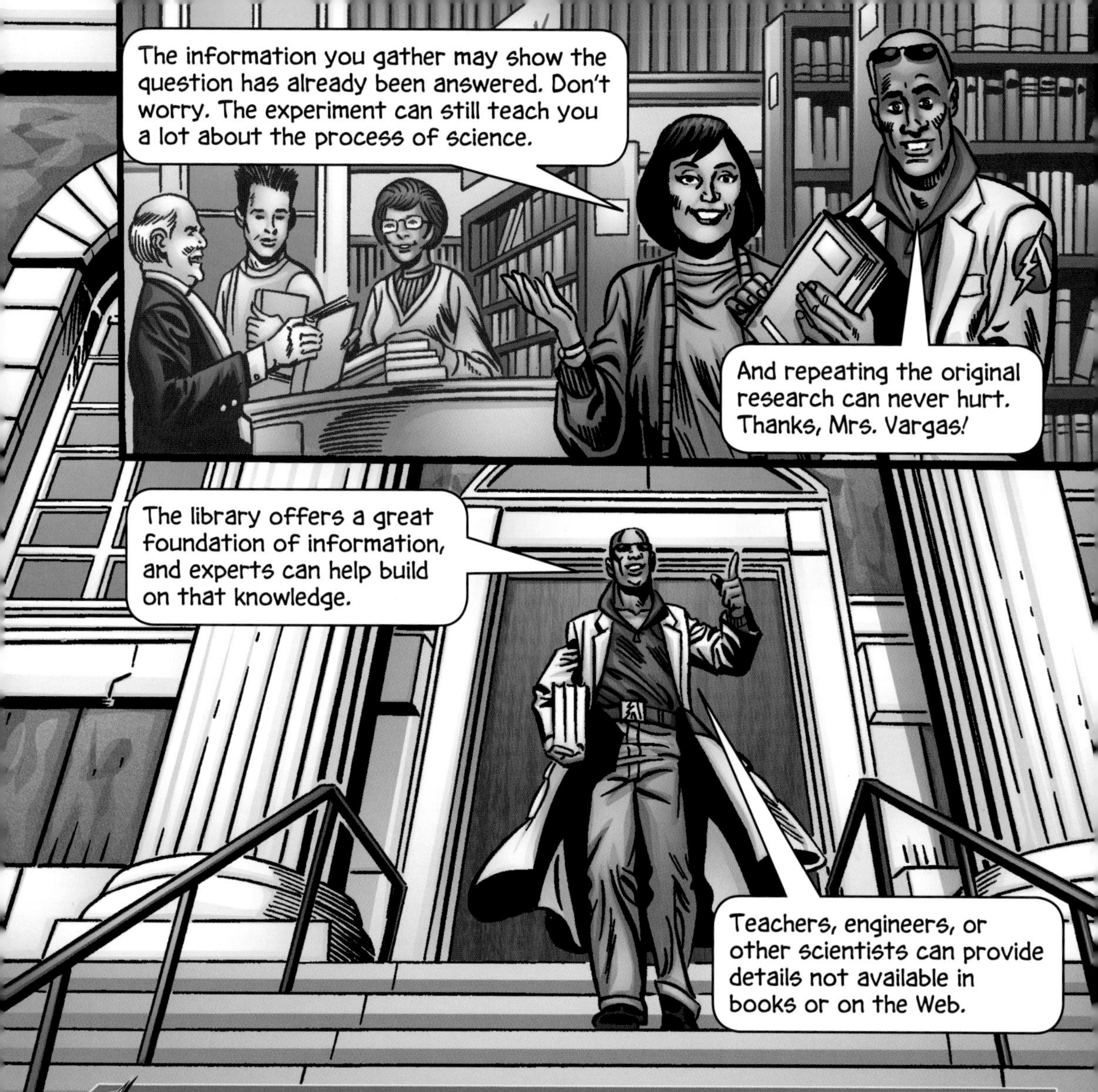

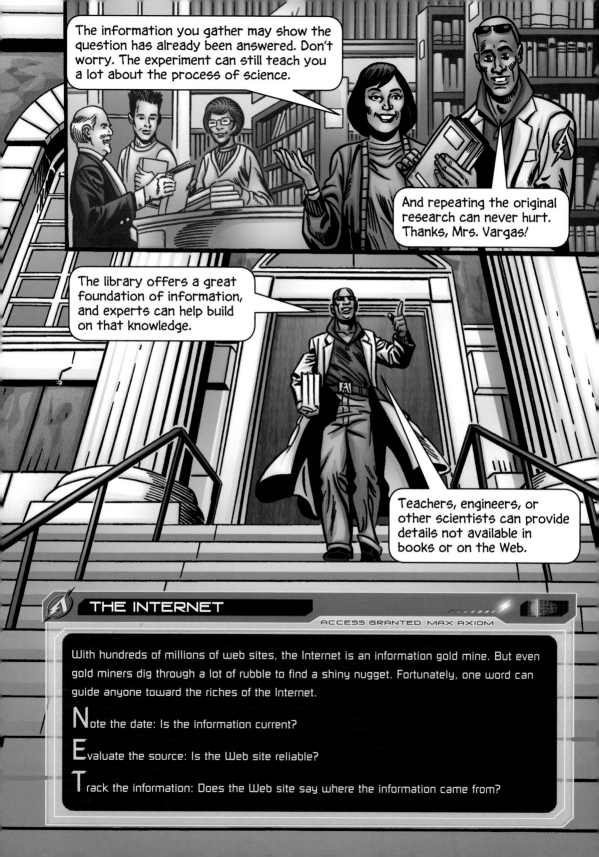

The information you gather may show the question has already been answered. Don't worry. The experiment can still teach you a lot about the process of science.
And repeating the original research can never hurt. Thanks, Mrs. Vargas!
The library offers a great foundation of information, and experts can help build on that knowledge.
Teachers, engineers, or other scientists can provide details not available in books or on the Web.

THE INTERNET

ACCESS GRANTED: MAX AXIOM

With hundreds of millions of web sites, the Internet is an information gold mine. But even gold miners dig through a lot of rubble to find a shiny nugget. Fortunately, one word can guide anyone toward the riches of the Internet.

Note the date: Is the information current?

Evaluate the source: Is the Web site reliable?

Track the information: Does the Web site say where the information came from?

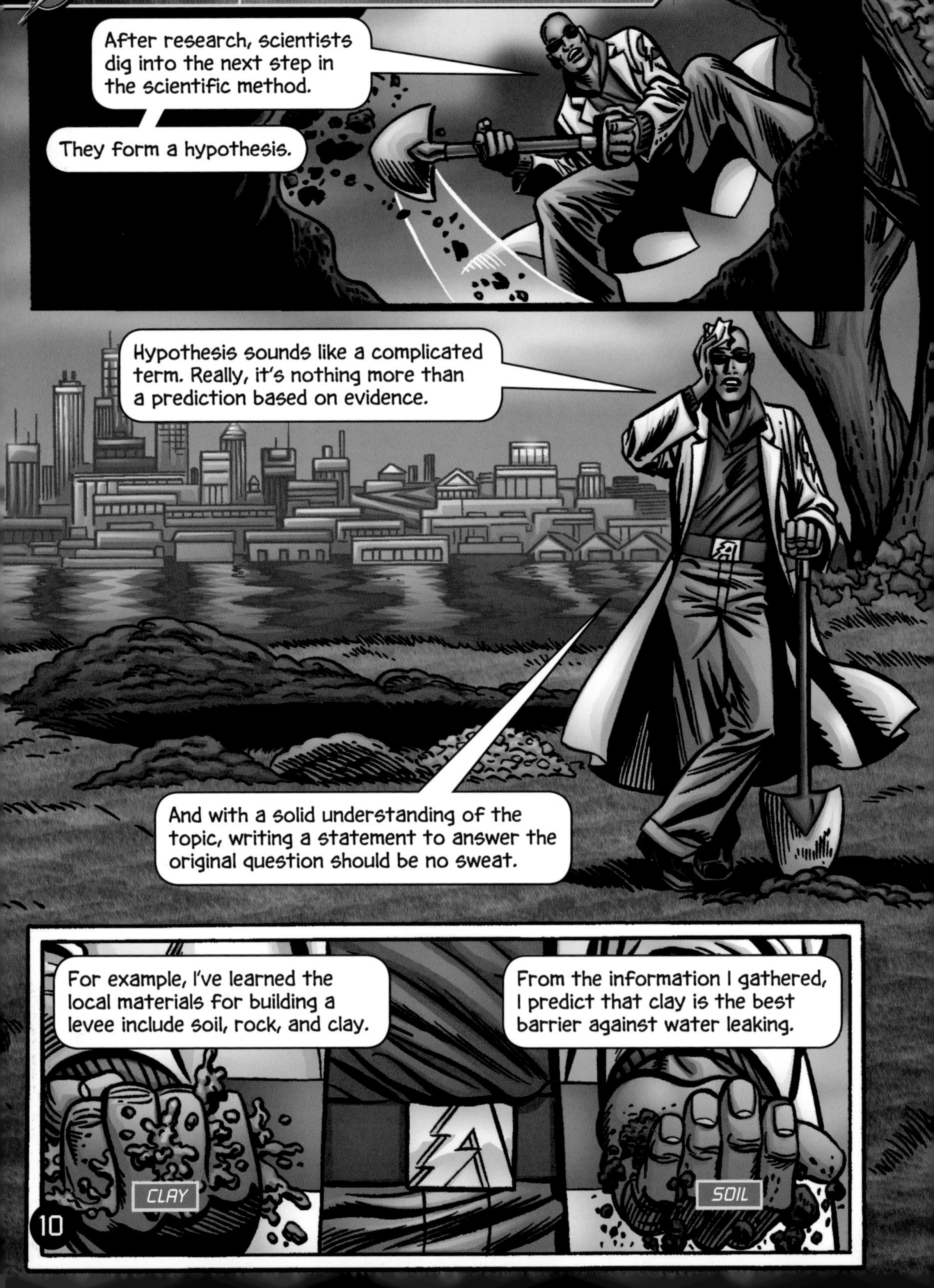
After research, scientists dig into the next step in the scientific method.
They form a hypothesis.
Hypothesis sounds like a complicated term. Really, it's nothing more than a prediction based on evidence.
And with a solid understanding of the topic, writing a statement to answer the original question should be no sweat.
For example, I've learned the local materials for building a levee include soil, rock, and clay.
From the information I gathered, I predict that clay is the best barrier against water leaking.
CLAY
SOIL

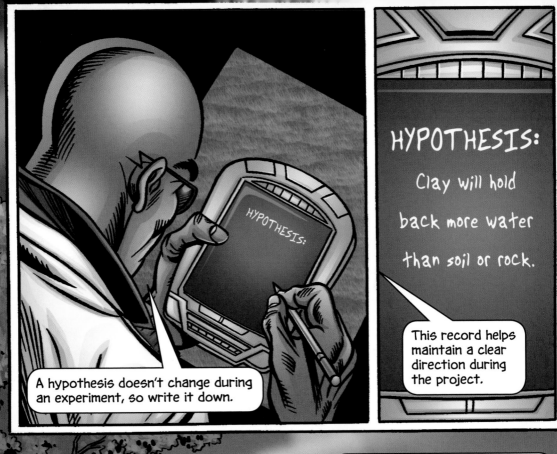

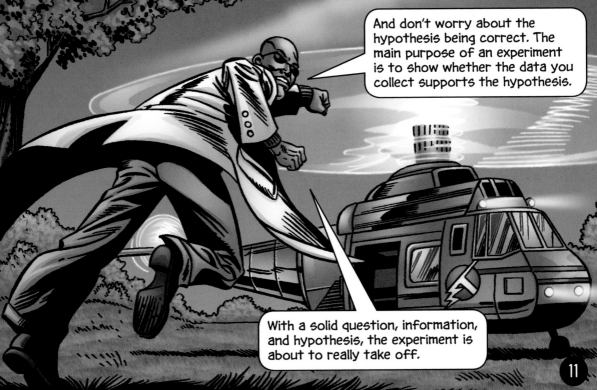

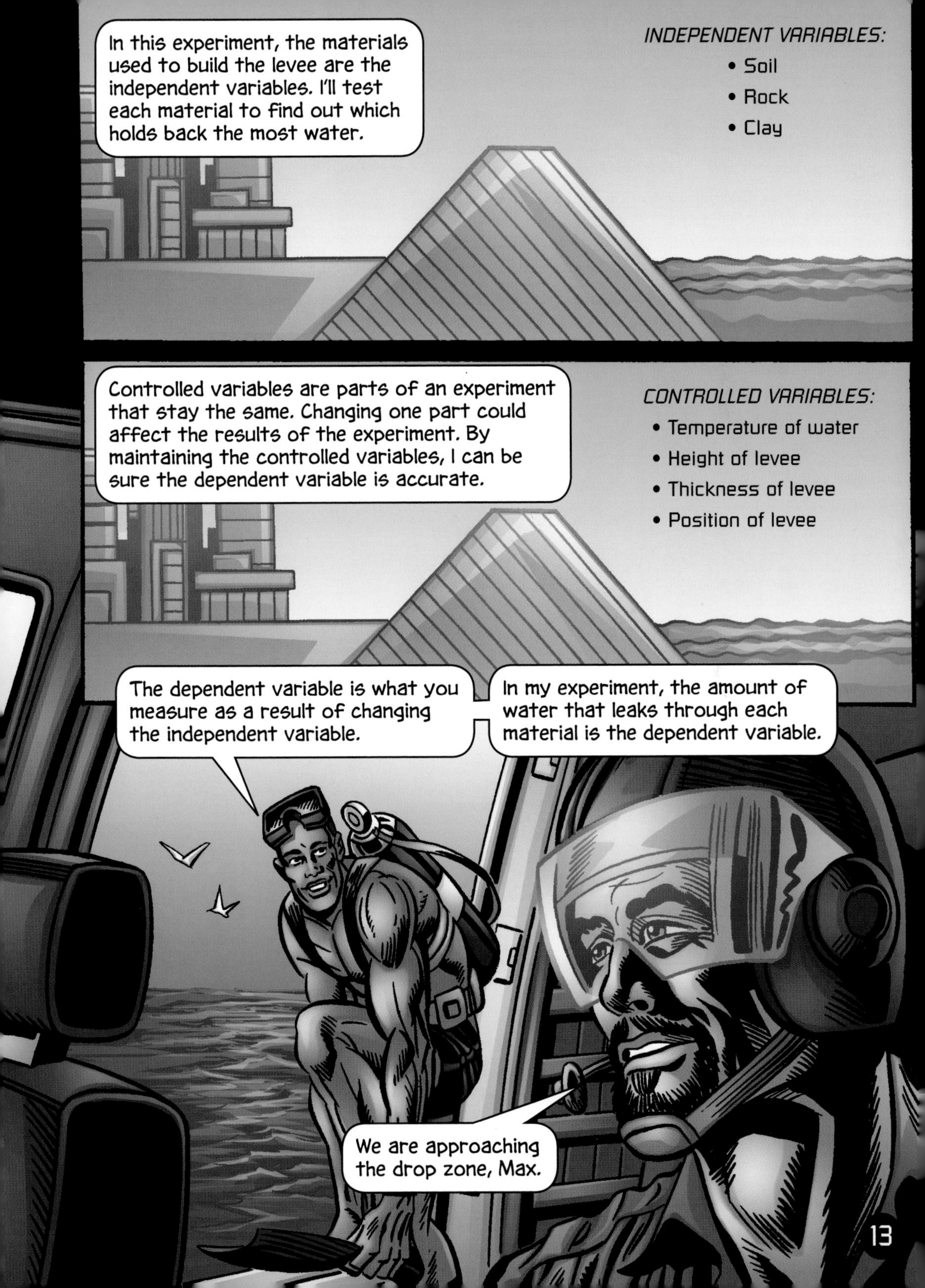
In this experiment, the materials used to build the levee are the independent variables. I'll test each material to find out which holds back the most water.
INDEPENDENT VARIABLES:
• Soil
• Rock
• Clay
Controlled variables are parts of an experiment that stay the same. Changing one part could affect the results of the experiment. By maintaining the controlled variables, I can be sure the dependent variable is accurate.
CONTROLLED VARIABLES:
• Temperature of water
• Height of levee
• Thickness of levee
• Position of levee
The dependent variable is what you measure as a result of changing the independent variable.
In my experiment, the amount of water that leaks through each material is the dependent variable.
We are approaching the drop zone, Max.

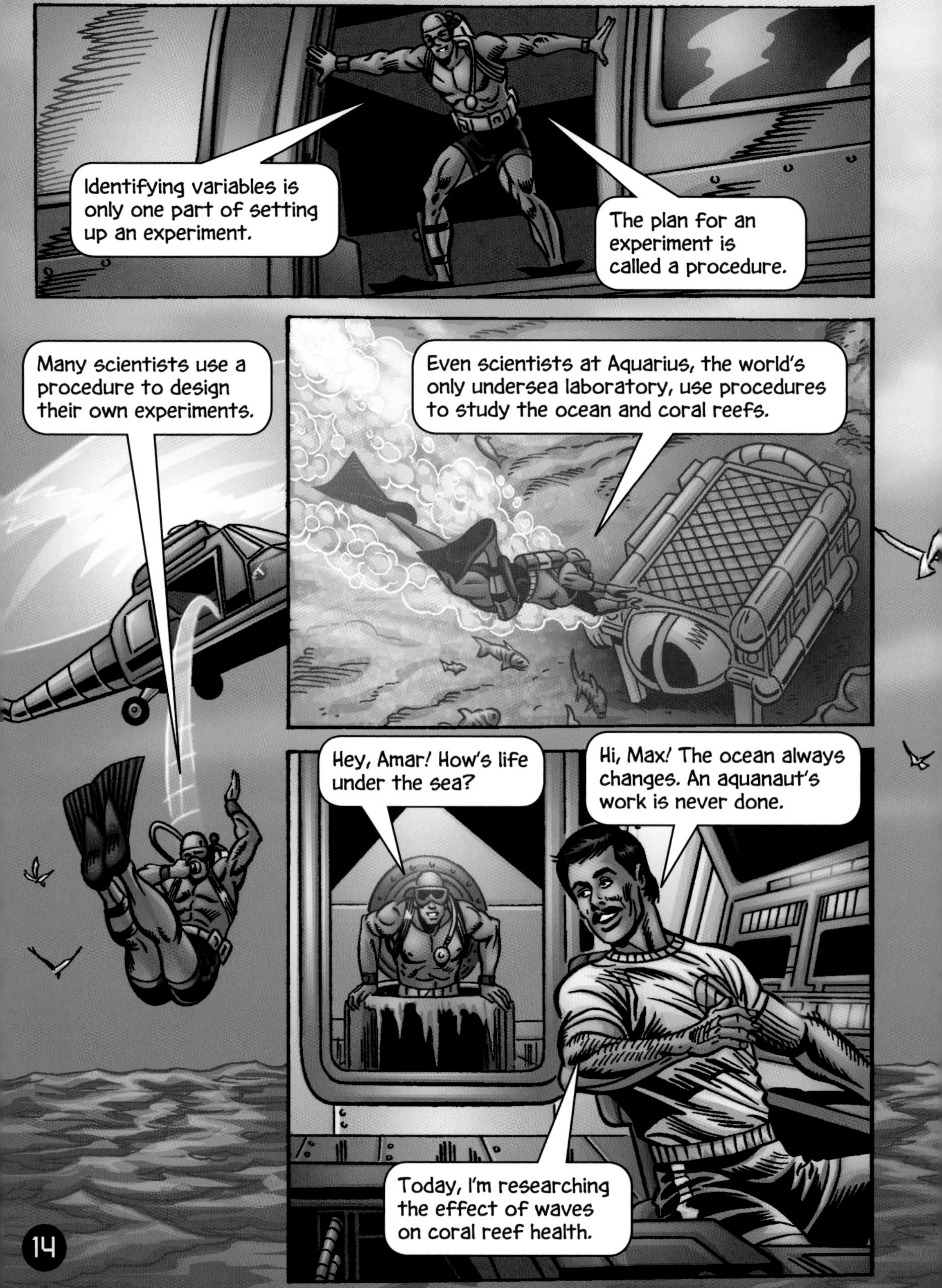
Identifying variables is only one part of setting up an experiment.
The plan for an experiment is called a procedure.
Many scientists use a procedure to design their own experiments.
Even scientists at Aquarius, the world's only undersea laboratory, use procedures to study the ocean and coral reefs.
Hey, Amar! How's life under the sea?
Hi, Max! The ocean always changes. An aquanaut's work is never done.
Today, I'm researching the effect of waves on coral reef health.

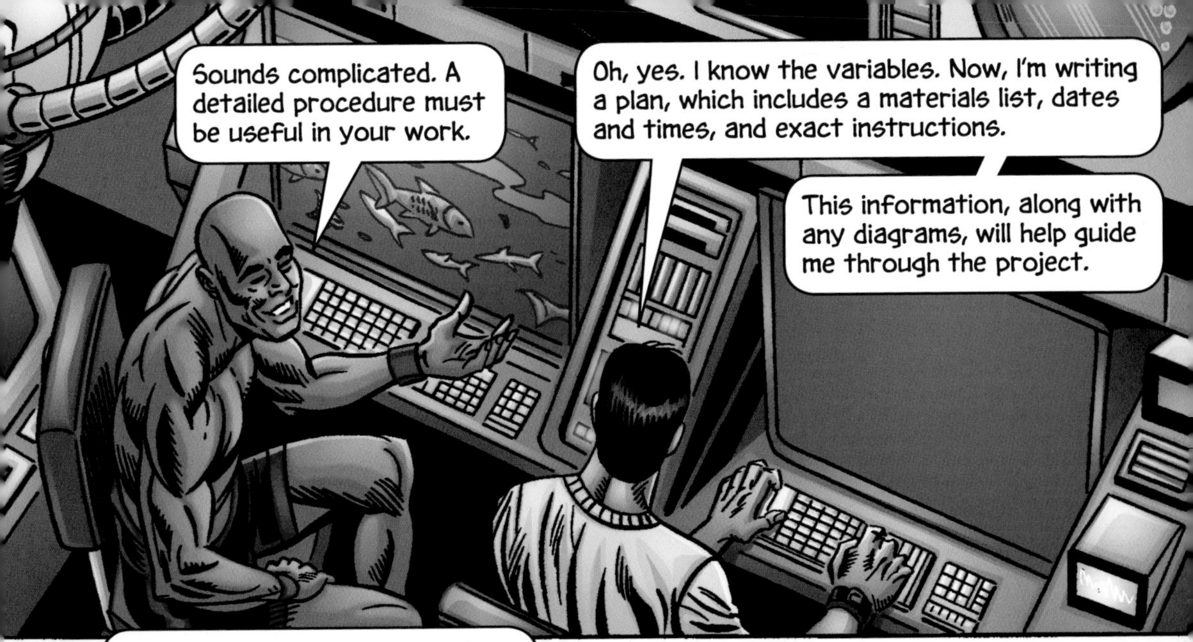
Sounds complicated. A detailed procedure must be useful in your work.
Oh, yes. I know the variables. Now, I'm writing a plan, which includes a materials list, dates and times, and exact instructions.
This information, along with any diagrams, will help guide me through the project.

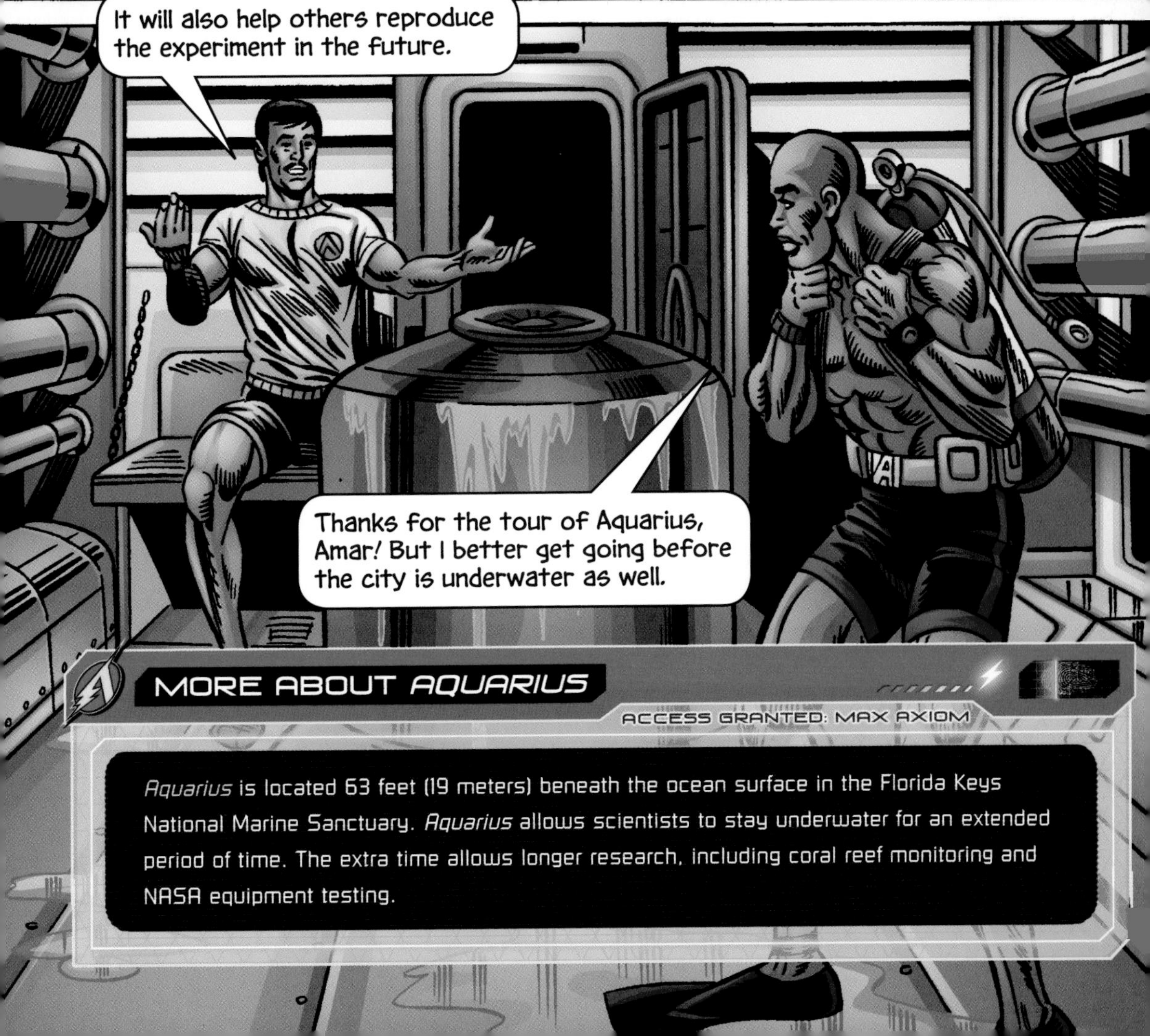
It will also help others reproduce the experiment in the future.
Thanks for the tour of Aquarius, Amar! But I better get going before the city is underwater as well.

MORE ABOUT *AQUARIUS*

ACCESS GRANTED: MAX AXIOM

Aquarius is located 63 feet (19 meters) beneath the ocean surface in the Florida Keys National Marine Sanctuary. *Aquarius* allows scientists to stay underwater for an extended period of time. The extra time allows longer research, including coral reef monitoring and NASA equipment testing.

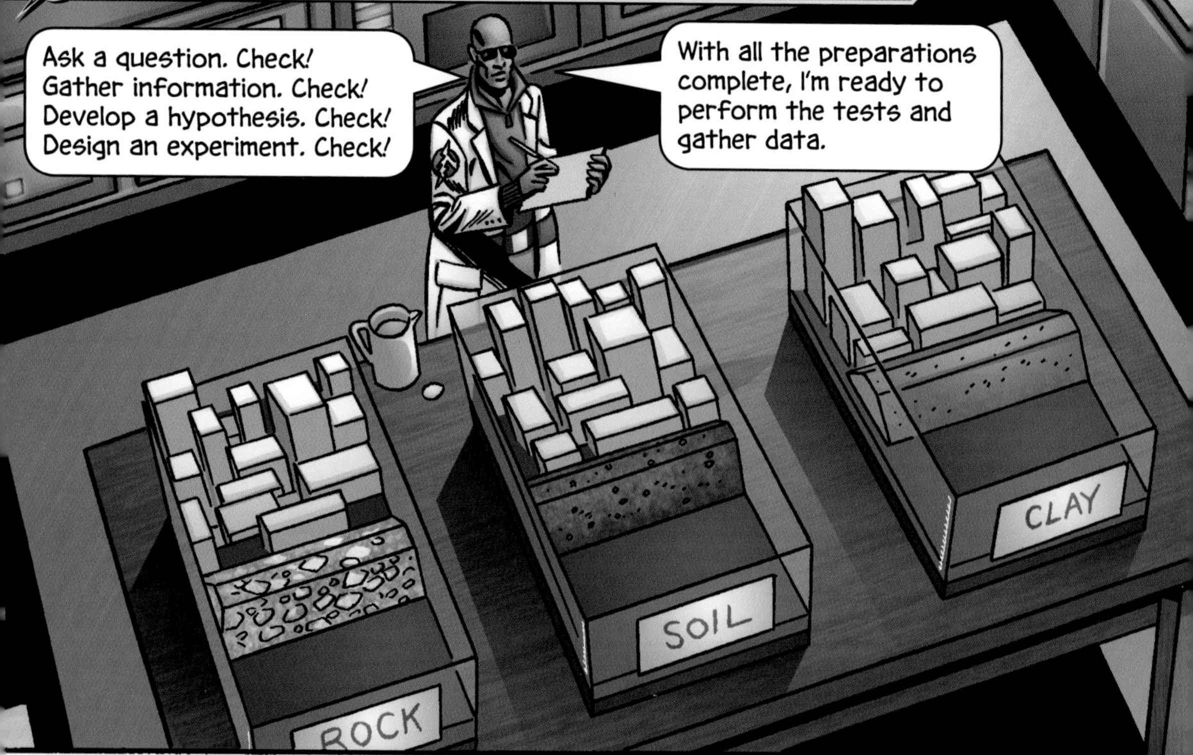
Ask a question. Check!
Gather information. Check!
Develop a hypothesis. Check!
Design an experiment. Check!
With all the preparations complete, I'm ready to perform the tests and gather data.
ROCK
SOIL
CLAY

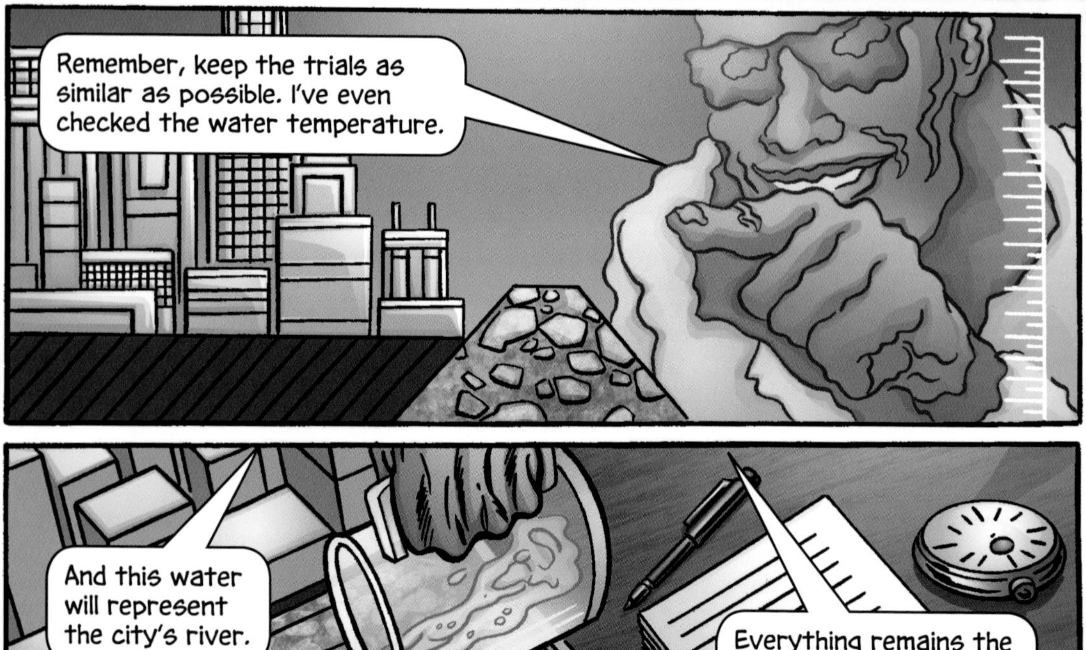
Remember, keep the trials as similar as possible. I've even checked the water temperature.

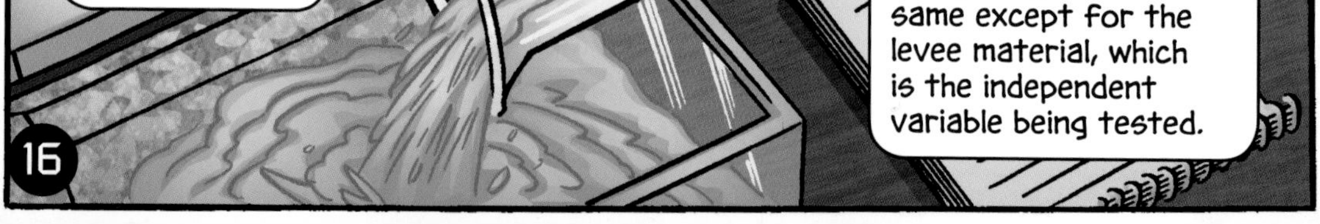
And this water will represent the city's river.
Everything remains the same except for the levee material, which is the independent variable being tested.

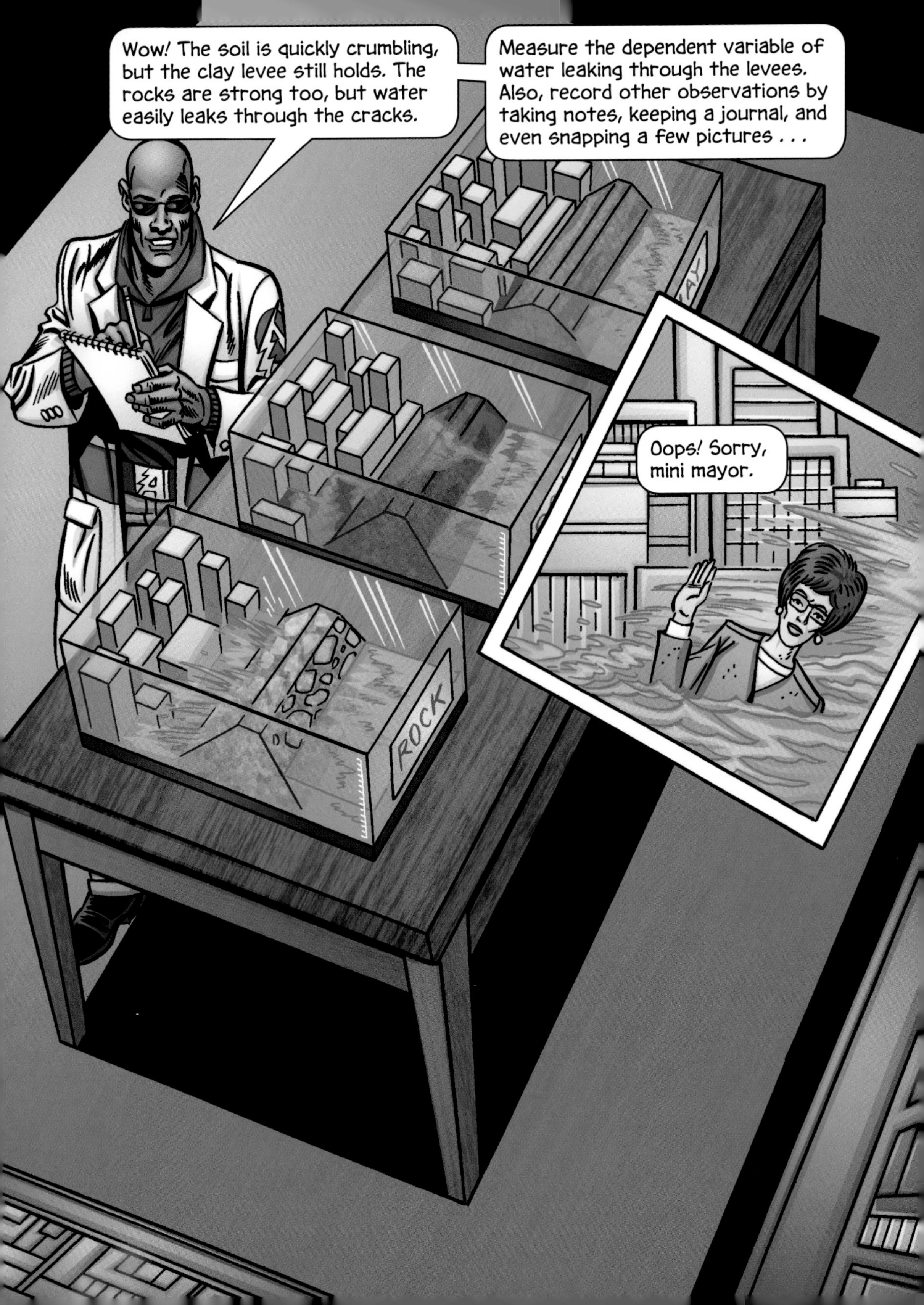
Wow! The soil is quickly crumbling, but the clay levee still holds. The rocks are strong too, but water easily leaks through the cracks.
Measure the dependent variable of water leaking through the levees. Also, record other observations by taking notes, keeping a journal, and even snapping a few pictures . . .
Oops! Sorry, mini mayor.
ROCK

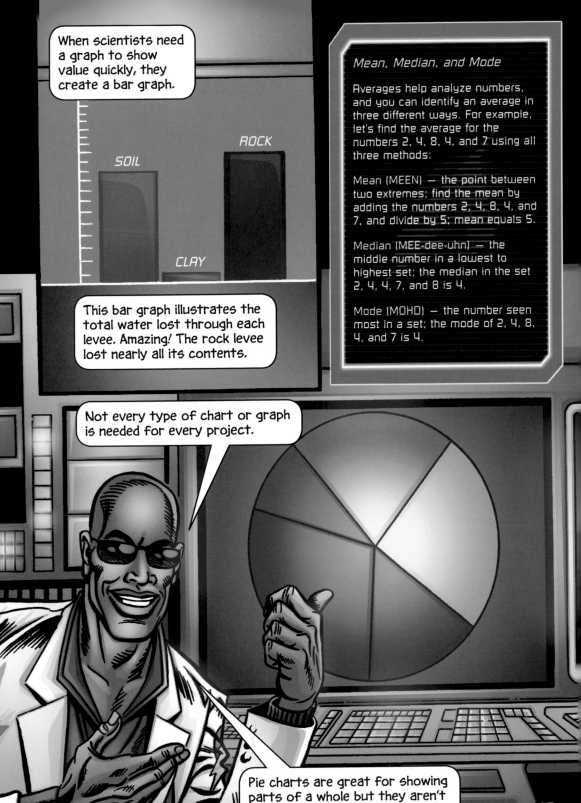

When scientists need a graph to show value quickly, they create a bar graph.

ROCK

SOIL

CLAY

This bar graph illustrates the total water lost through each levee. Amazing! The rock levee lost nearly all its contents.

Mean, Median, and Mode

Averages help analyze numbers, and you can identify an average in three different ways. For example, let's find the average for the numbers 2, 4, 8, 4, and 7 using all three methods:

Mean (MEEN) — the point between two extremes; find the mean by adding the numbers 2, 4, 8, 4, and 7, and divide by 5; mean equals 5.

Median (MEE-dee-uhn) — the middle number in a lowest to highest set; the median in the set 2, 4, 4, 7, and 8 is 4.

Mode (MOHD) — the number seen most in a set; the mode of 2, 4, 8, 4, and 7 is 4.

Not every type of chart or graph is needed for every project.

Pie charts are great for showing parts of a whole but they aren't necessary for this experiment.

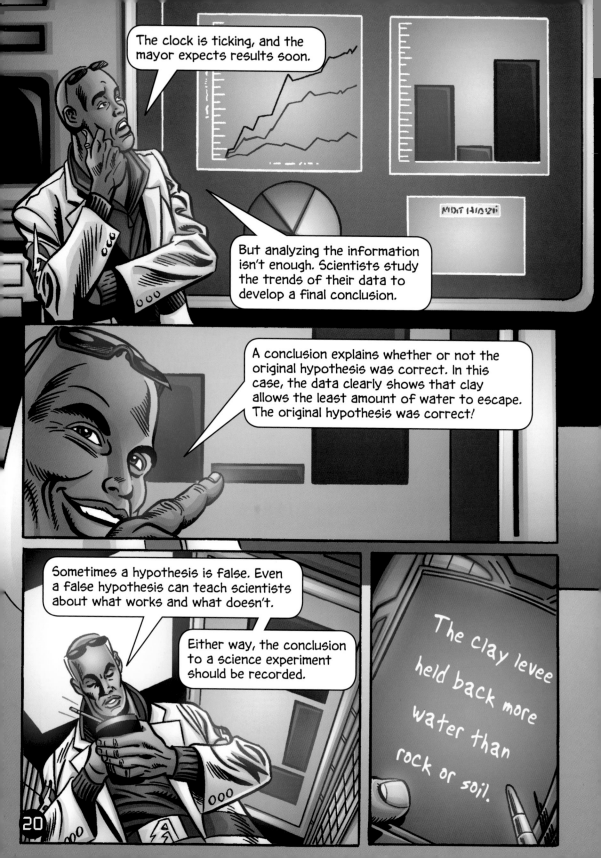

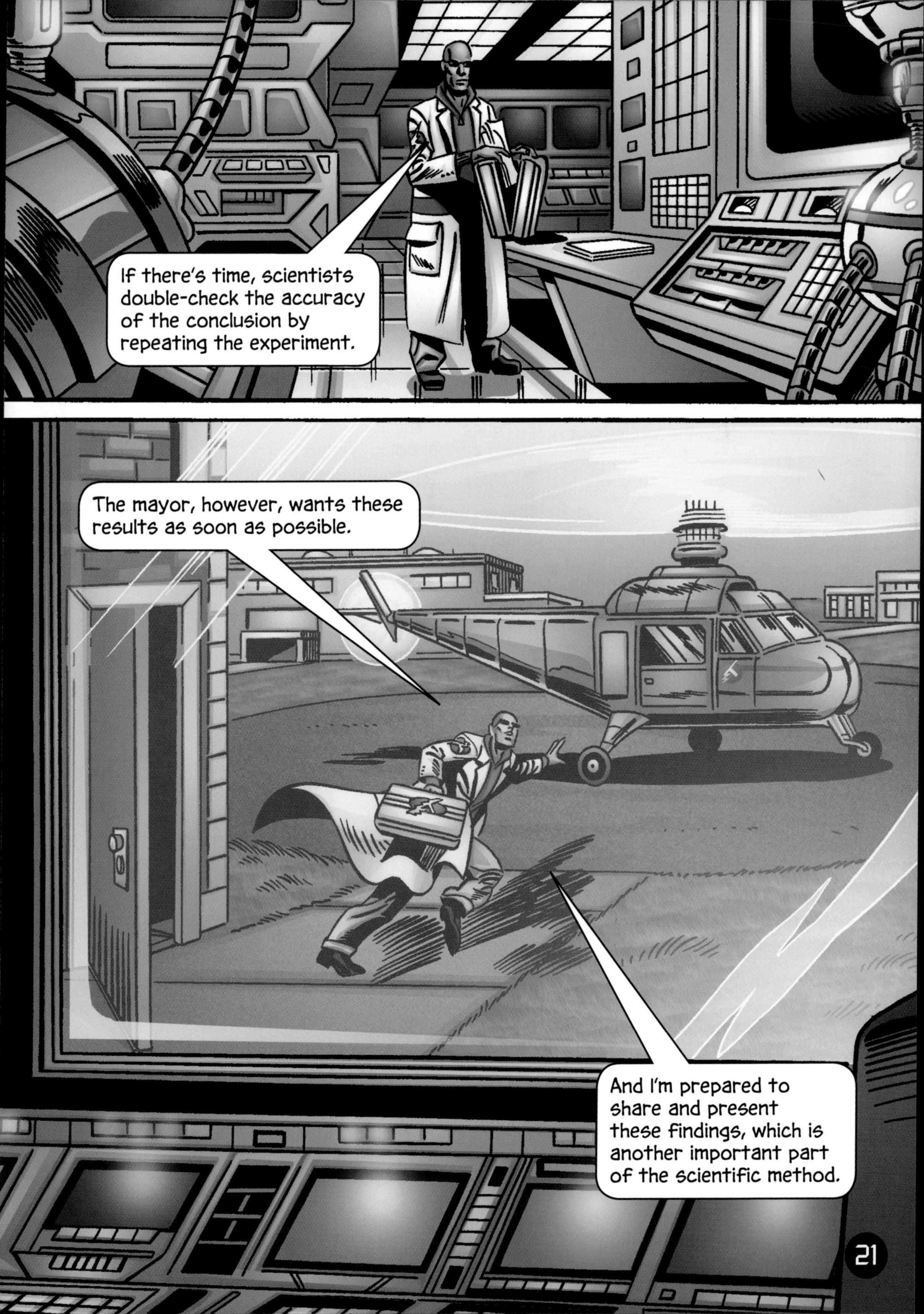
If there's time, scientists double-check the accuracy of the conclusion by repeating the experiment.
The mayor, however, wants these results as soon as possible.
And I'm prepared to share and present these findings, which is another important part of the scientific method.

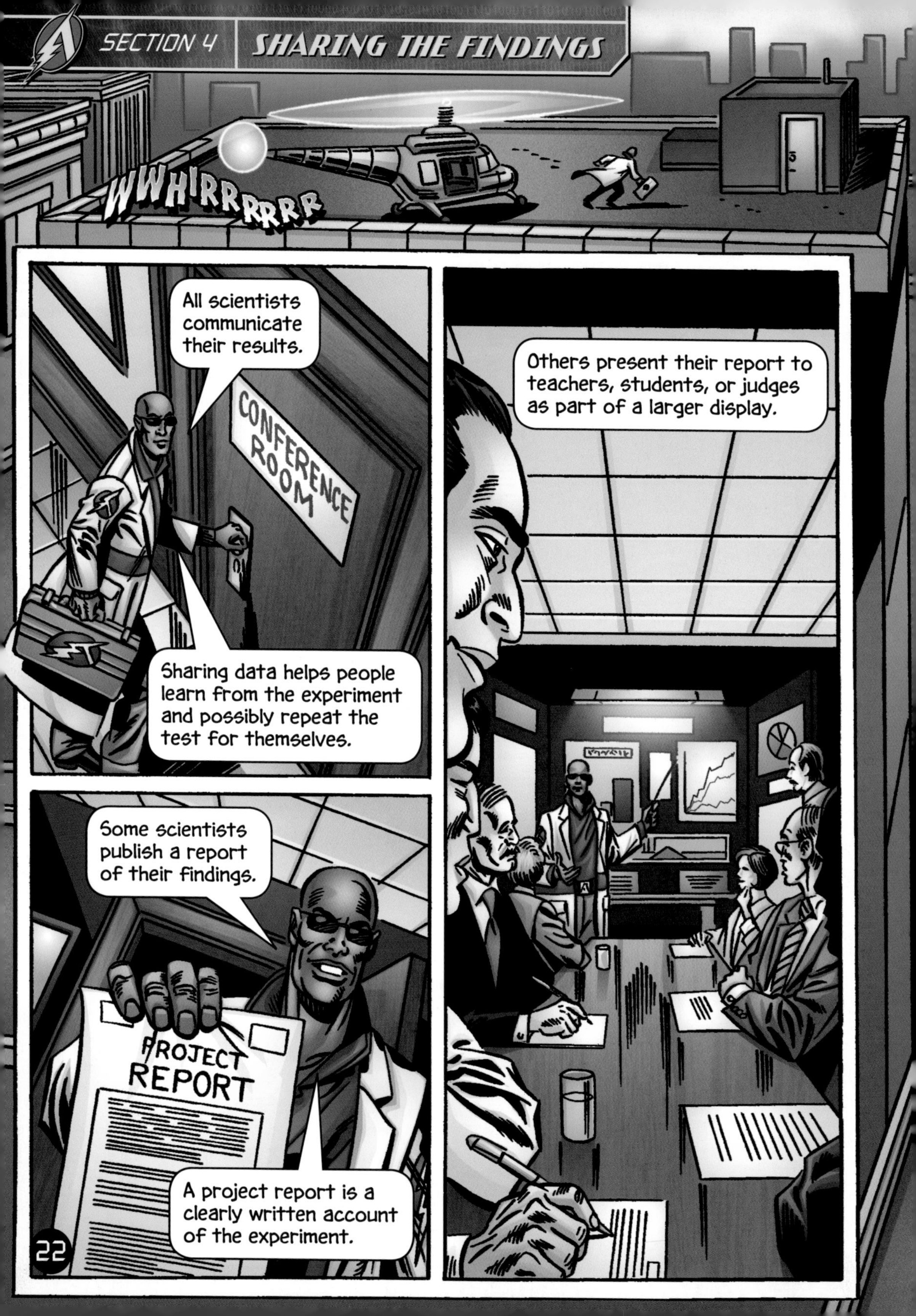

SECTION 4
SHARING THE FINDINGS
WWHIRRRRRRR
All scientists communicate their results.
CONFERENCE ROOM
Sharing data helps people learn from the experiment and possibly repeat the test for themselves.
Some scientists publish a report of their findings.
PROJECT REPORT
A project report is a clearly written account of the experiment.
Others present their report to teachers, students, or judges as part of a larger display.

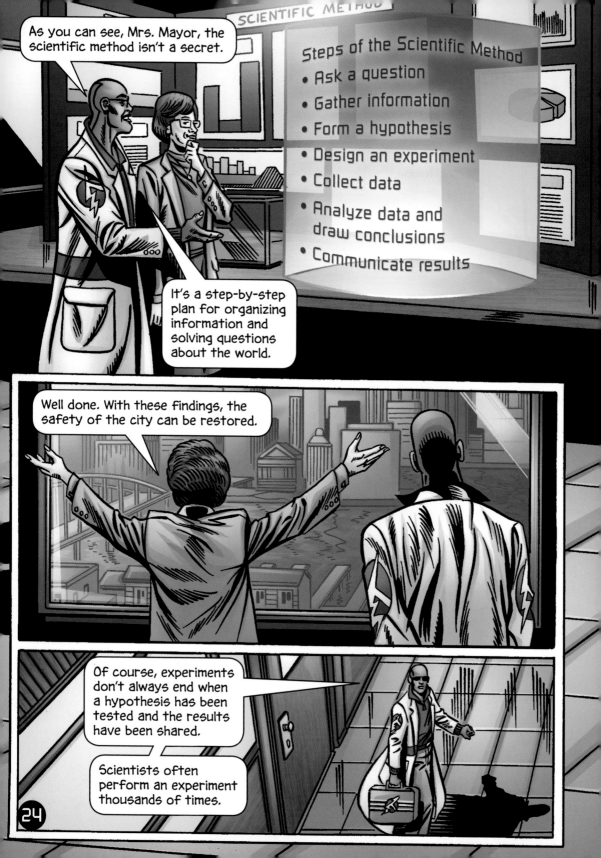

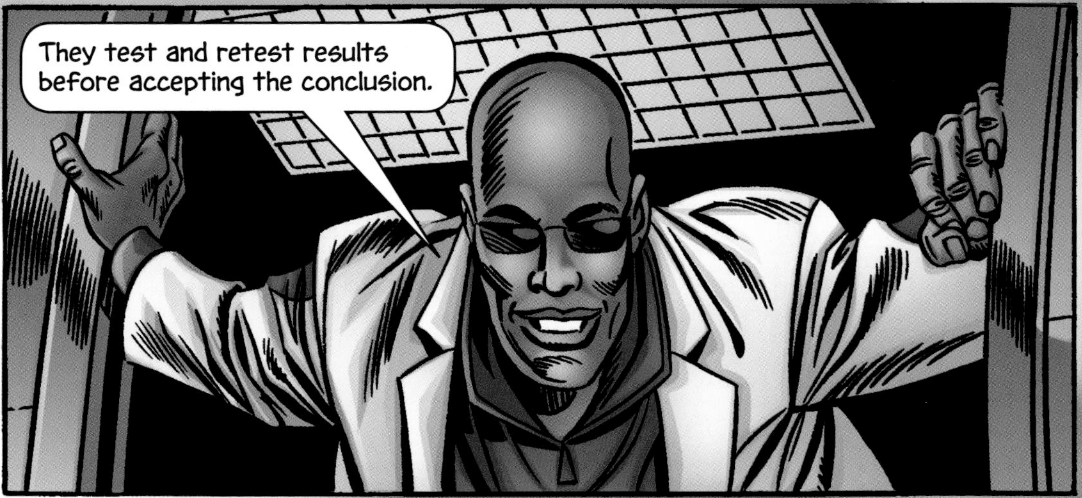
They test and retest results before accepting the conclusion.

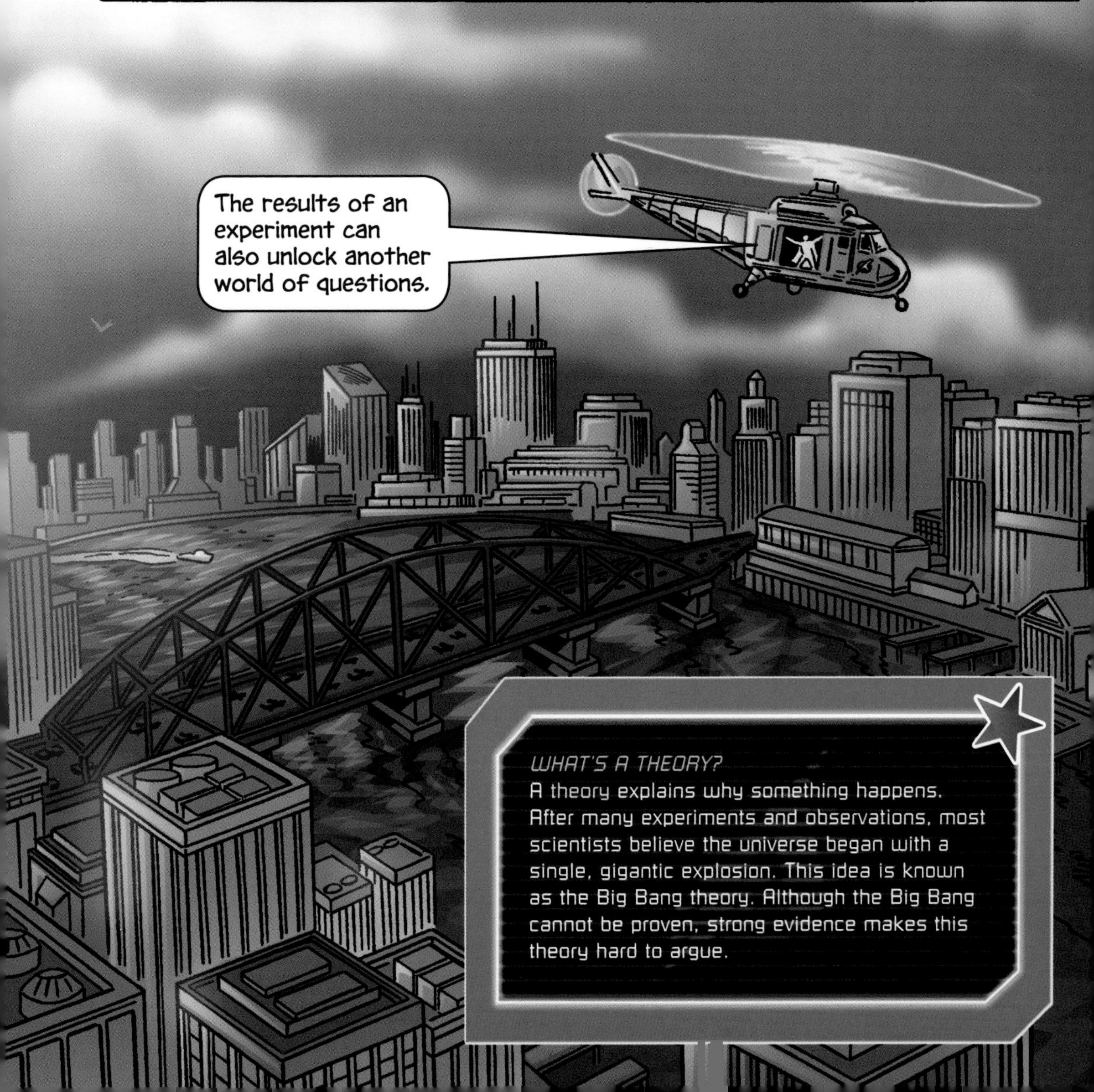
The results of an experiment can also unlock another world of questions.

WHAT'S A THEORY?

A theory explains why something happens. After many experiments and observations, most scientists believe the universe began with a single, gigantic explosion. This idea is known as the Big Bang theory. Although the Big Bang cannot be proven, strong evidence makes this theory hard to argue.

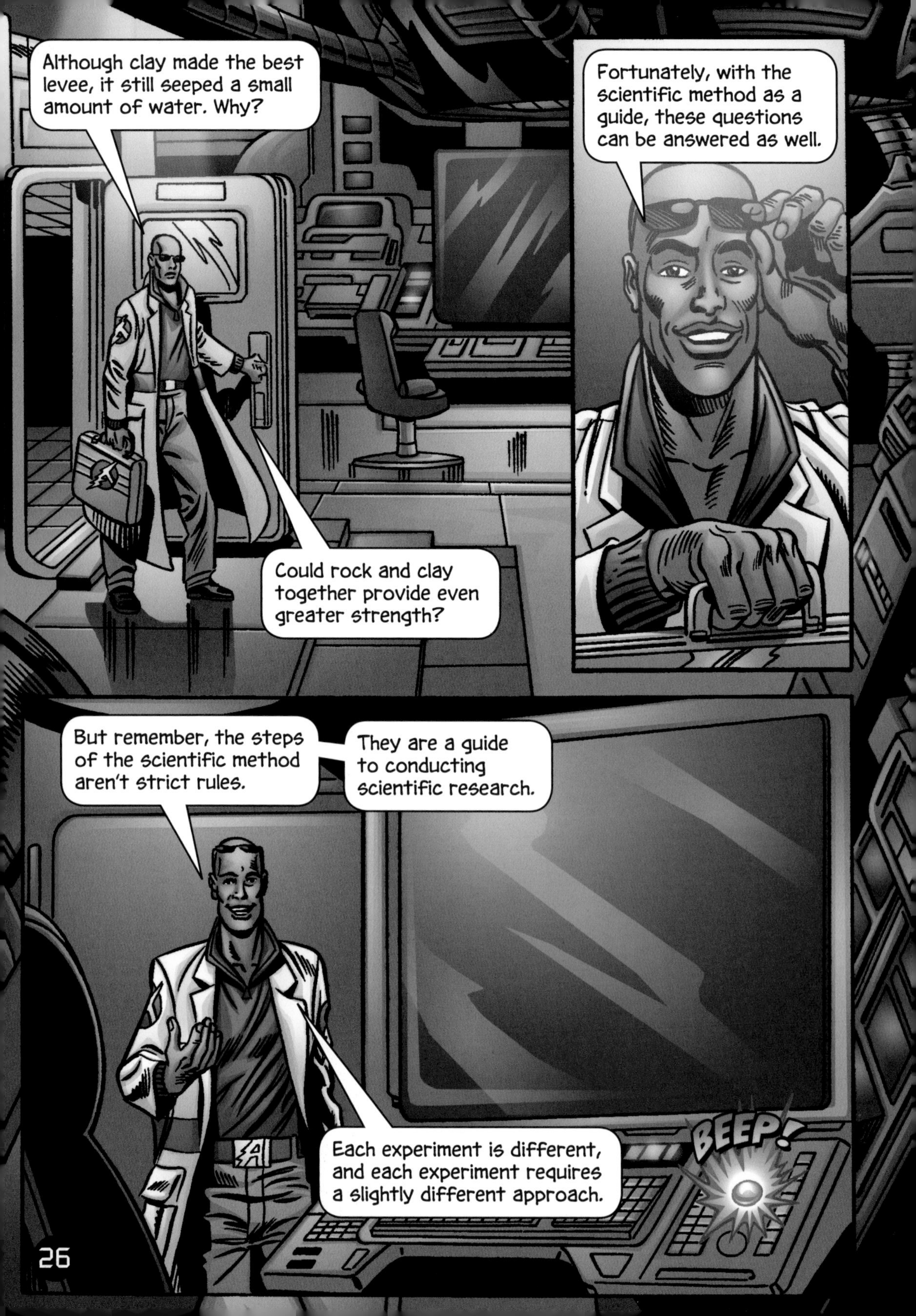

Although clay made the best levee, it still seeped a small amount of water. Why?
Could rock and clay together provide even greater strength?
Fortunately, with the scientific method as a guide, these questions can be answered as well.
But remember, the steps of the scientific method aren't strict rules.
They are a guide to conducting scientific research.
Each experiment is different, and each experiment requires a slightly different approach.
BEEP!

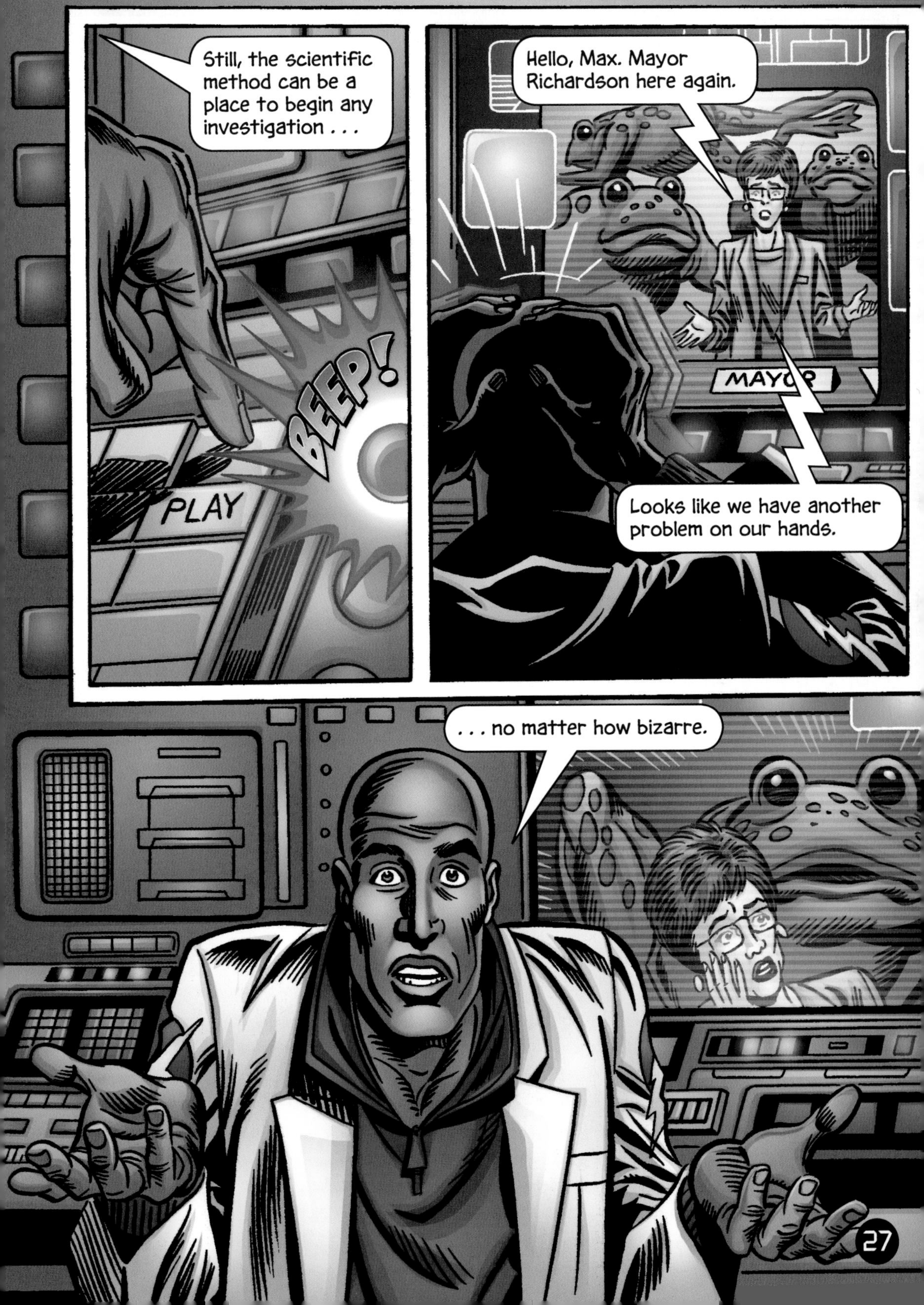
Still, the scientific method can be a place to begin any investigation . . .
BEEP!
PLAY
Hello, Max. Mayor Richardson here again.
MAYOR
Looks like we have another problem on our hands.
. . . no matter how bizarre.

MORE ABOUT THE
SCIENTIFIC METHOD

No one knows who developed the scientific method. But many people believe Francesco Redi performed the first experiment to match this process. In 1668, most scientists believed maggots grew directly from rotten meat. Redi, however, believed maggots hatched from fly eggs. He proved this idea correct by forming a hypothesis, designing an experiment, and analyzing the data.

Scientists work in many fields and don't always answer their questions in the same way. An astronomer investigates questions about the universe in ways that differ from a chemist discovering the structure of matter. Some scientists conduct experimental studies while others rely on interviews. The methods scientists use to gather data depend on the questions they are trying to answer.

With more than 130 million items, the Library of Congress in Washington, D.C., is the largest library in the world. It has more than 530 miles (853 kilometers) of bookshelves! But like most libraries today, many of the Library of Congress' resources are available on the Internet.

Scientists often test large experiments on miniature models. In the early 1900s, inventors Wilbur and Orville Wright tested more than 200 miniature airplane wings inside their 16-inch (41-centimeter) wide wind tunnel. After finding the best design, the inventors built full-size versions of the wings. On December 17, 1903, their wings made history as part of the first powered airplane to take flight.

The International Science and Engineering Fair (ISEF) is the largest science competition for students in the world. Each year, the ISEF awards more than $4 million in scholarships and prizes to its top competitors.

Aquanauts experiment inside *Aquarius*, but scientists studying space head to the *International Space Station*. This giant series of modules orbits 250 miles (400 km) above the earth. Scientists from around the globe, including U.S. astronauts, use the station as a laboratory and observatory.

EARTHEN LEVEE

Max used the scientific method to learn about the best materials for building an earthen levee. Now you can build a levee of your own!

WHAT YOU NEED:

- scissors
- egg carton
- large container with a smooth bottom
- gravel
- sand
- water
- pottery clay
- rolling pin

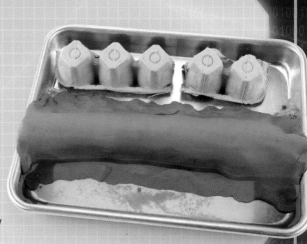

WHAT YOU DO:

1. Using a scissors, cut off four or five egg cups from the egg carton. Place these upside down on one side of the large container. They represent buildings in a floodplain.

2. Create a wall of gravel 2 to 3 inches (5 to 7 cm) high down the center of the container.

3. Mix a small amount of water with the sand to make it damp. Pack sand around the gravel wall.

4. Roll and pat the clay into a flat sheet long enough and wide enough to cover the levee. Place the sheet over the levee. Smooth it and press its edges to the sides and bottom of the container to form a tight seal.

5. Slowly fill the side of the container opposite the egg cups with water to represent rising floodwaters.

6. Note areas where the wall is weak or leaky. Apply more gravel to make these parts of the wall stronger. Add clay to fill in leaks.

DISCUSSION QUESTIONS

1. Why is it important to write a detailed procedure for an experiment? What problems might arise if you didn't write a detailed procedure?

2. Max creates three model levees to conduct his experiment. Why is it important that they are exactly alike in all ways but one?

3. Which step of the scientific method is Max carrying out on pages 18 through 20? Why is this step important?

4. The last step of the scientific method is to communicate results. What are two ways scientists can do so?

WRITING PROMPTS

1. Write a paragraph that defines the differences between controlled variables, dependent variables, and independent variables.

2. The second step of the scientific method is to gather information. Make a list of all of the ways you could gather information about a science topic.

3. Imagine that you needed to conduct the same levee experiment Max does in this book. Write a paragraph describing how you would improve or change Max's experimental design.

4. Pretend you are the mayor and you need to call Max Axiom to solve a problem using the scientific method. Rewrite the mayor's dialogue on page 4 to give Max his new mission!

TAKE A QUIZ!

GLOSSARY

analyze (AN-uh-lize)—to examine something carefully in order to understand it

aquanaut (AK-wuh-nawt)—a scuba diver who lives and works inside and outside an underwater shelter for an extended period

conclusion (kuhn-KLOO-shuhn)—a decision or realization based on the facts available

controlled variable (kuhn-TROHLD VAIR-ee-uh-buhl)—a part of an experiment that stays the same

data (DAY-tuh)—information or facts

dependent variable (dee-PEN-duhnt VAIR-ee-uh-buhl)—a measured result of a change in the independent variable of an experiment

evidence (EV-uh-duhnss)—information, items, and facts that help prove something is true or false

hypothesis (hye-POTH-uh-siss)—a prediction that can be tested about how a scientific investigation or experiment will turn out

independent variable (in-di-PEN-duhnt VAIR-ee-uh-buhl)—a part of an experiment that changes

observation (ob-zur-VAY-shuhn)—something that you have noticed by watching carefully

prediction (pri-DIK-shuhn)—a statement of what you think will happen in the future; a hypothesis is a scientific prediction

procedure (pruh-SEE-jur)—a set way of doing something

research (REE-surch)—to study and learn about a subject

READ MORE

Flynn, Riley. *Asking Questions and Finding Solutions.* Science and Engineering Practices. North Mankato, Minn.: Capstone Press, 2017.

Hunter, Dru. *How Do We Apply Science?* Think Like a Scientist. Mankato, Minn.: Creative Education, 2016.

Leigh, Anna. *30-Minute Outdoor Science Projects.* 30-Minute Makers. Minneapolis: Lerner Publications, 2019.

Mould, Steve. *How to Be a Scientist.* New York: DK Publishing, 2017.

INTERNET SITES

Use Facthound to find Internet sites related to this book.

Visit *www.facthound.com*

Just type in 9781543558708 and go!

Check out projects, games and lots more at
www.capstonekids.com

INDEX